The History of the Sunni and Shia Split: Understanding the Divisions within Islam

By Dr. Jesse Harasta and Charles River Editors

A depiction of an angel presenting Muhammad with a miniature city

About Charles River Editors

Charles River Editors provides superior editing and original writing services across the digital publishing industry, with the expertise to create digital content for publishers across a vast range of subject matter. In addition to providing original digital content for third party publishers, we also republish civilization's greatest literary works, bringing them to new generations of readers via ebooks.

Sign up here to receive updates about free books as we publish them, and visit Our Kindle Author Page to browse today's free promotions and our most recently published Kindle titles.

Introduction

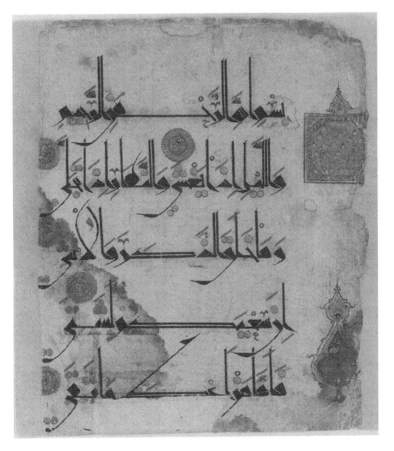

A medieval manuscript depicting the Qur'an.

The Sunni and Shia

Different branches of the same religion are the exception more than the rule, and they have had a profound impact upon history. The schism between the Orthodox and Catholic Churches influenced relationships between nations across Europe, and religious intolerance based on different Christian faiths led to persecution and outright violence across the continent for centuries. The Protestant Reformation split Christianity further, and the results culminated in the incredibly destructive Thirty Years' War in the 17th century.

Today, the most important religious split is between the Sunnis and the Shias (Shiites) within Islam. Unlike divisions in other faiths - between Conservative and Orthodox Jews or Catholic and Protestant Christians - the split between the Sunnis and Shia has existed almost as long as the faith itself, and it quickly emerged out of tensions created by the political crisis after the death of the Prophet Muhammad. In a sense, what are now two different forms of Islam essentially started as political factions within the unified body of Muslim believers.

Over the past few centuries, Christians have mostly been able to live alongside their co-religionists, but the split between the Sunnis and Shias is still so pronounced that many adherents of each branch view each other with disdain if not as outright apostates or non-believers. The religious divide is perhaps the most important fault line in the turbulent Middle East today, with Sunni nations like Egypt and Saudi Arabia at odds with Shiite nations like Iran. At lower levels, non-state groups like the Islamic State and Hezbollah are fighting each other in ways that cross state lines in places like Lebanon, Iraq, and Syria. Although it is technically a split in religion, the divide has had substantial global ramifications for decades, and there seems to be no end in sight.

The History of the Sunni and Shia Split traces the origins of the split and the historic effects of the main divide within Islam. Along with pictures of important people, places, and events, you will learn about the history of the Sunnis and Shias like never before, in no time at all.

The History of the Sunni and Shia Split: Understanding the Divisions Within Islam

About Charles River Editors

Introduction

A Note on Christian versus Muslim Dates

Since this book is written for mostly non-Muslim readers familiar with the globally accepted Christian-derived dating system, it uses BCE and CE as dates, based upon the estimated year of the birth of Jesus Christ. While Muslims recognize Jesus as a prophet, they do not base their calendar upon his birth but instead upon the year when their Prophet, Muhammad, made his triumphant return pilgrimage to Mecca. This year, which falls on the Christian year 622 CE, is considered Year One of the Anno Hegirae (AH) system. That said, BCE/CE system is used throughout this book to avoid confusion, and dates can be converted to AH if necessary by subtracting 622 years.

Comparing Sunnis and Shias to Christians

When the European colonial powers, especially Britain, first began to attempt to govern conquered sections of the Muslim world, they created a class of "Orientalists," scholars who specialized in studying and explaining the Orient to the colonial government. A metaphor that they developed at that time which has taken deep roots in Western thought on the subject of the Muslim denominations was that Sunnis were like Protestants and Shias were like Catholics. They pointed to the emphasis Shias put on following their priesthood, on rituals, and upon mysticism, and the scholars saw this as having parallels in Catholic practice. In contrast, they viewed the emphasis of the Sunnis on rationalism and their long history of scientific accomplishment as similar to the Protestants.

There are a number of problems with this comparison that make it basically useless. The first is that the patriotic Britons who created this comparison themselves saw Protestants as naturally being more rational, intelligent and superior to Catholics, a perspective that is today understood to be a product of British nationalist imaginations. The second is that the comparison clearly doesn't go below the surface; unlike the Protestants, the Sunnis did not break free from a Shia-dominated religious establishment, and the Shia have never been dominant numerically. Furthermore, while the Sunni thinkers do have a long history of rational thought and exploration of the natural world, the same can be said of Shia thinkers, especially from Persia, and their system of jurisprudence is as much based upon the rational analysis and careful debate and study of texts as the Sunnis'. While certain radical Sunni groups (such as the Wahhabis) violently reject the ritual elements of the Islamic tradition, in truth the Sunni world also has a rich history of such practices, though they may not be as open and dramatic as the Shia Ashura festival.

When exploring the Sunni and Shia split, it is better not to make comparisons to Christians or other groups but instead attempt to understand the differences based upon their own terms. With over a billion Muslims in the world, they clearly warrant their own treatment, their own categories, and their own history.

Chapter 1: The Seeds of Conflict and the Death of the Prophet

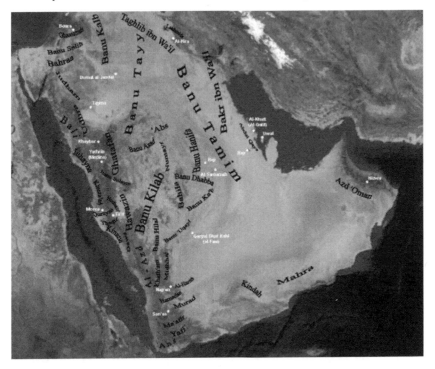

The Arabian Peninsula and the names of various tribes during Muhammad's life

The split between the two forms of Islam was already in the process of forming upon the death of the Prophet Muhammad. Muhammad had constructed around himself not only a potent new religious movement but also a powerful young state called the Ummah (the "Community" for lack of a better translation). Belonging to the Islamic faith also meant belonging to the Ummah, which was governed by its own laws and had many of its own institutions. In his own lifetime, Muhammad had ruled the Ummah through what sociologists call "charismatic authority," a term coined by Max Weber that is defined as "resting on devotion to the exceptional sanctity, heroism or exemplary character of an individual person, and of the normative patterns or order revealed or ordained by him." Hence, Muslims believe Muhammad ruled because he was uniquely chosen and endowed by God as the exemplar of all humanity, giving him a unique (though not perfect or infallible) ability to govern humanity. This was a holistic form of governance because the Prophet did not simply deliver God's words (what became the Holy Qur'an), nor did he simply pronounce upon court cases and create laws. He did all those things, but he also presented in his own person the embodiment of the best that humanity could aspire to. He was fully human, but the finest, most pious example that humans would ever produce[1].

One of the problems with charismatic authority, as Max Weber recognized and pointed out, is that charismatic authority is fragile because it cannot last beyond the lifespan of the charismatic individual without major changes. As a result, it is often difficult to create continuity after the death of a charismatic leader. Plenty of societies or movements have experienced collapse or massive upheaval after the death of a charismatic leader, such as France after Napoleon and the ancient world after Alexander the Great.

The process of converting a charismatic authority into a more stable, long-term form of government is called "routinizing charisma." In this process, the society attempts to keep some of the legitimizing elements of the deceased leader in place while also creating ways to choose new leaders. This can be agonizing, especially since new leaders rarely live up to or replace the one who has come before. That said, history has provided several successful examples, such as the Roman Empire after Julius Caesar, the Christian Church after Jesus, and the Islamic Republic of Iran after Ayatollah Khomeini.

The Ummah understood that once Muhammad died, he could not be truly replaced and that there would never again be a man like him. That said, the Ummah hoped to find a leader that was still significantly superior to the ordinary man, and the most obvious candidates for superior people were the Prophet's family. Was there some way that the special qualities of Muhammad could be found amongst the members of his close family? Was there some special teaching or insight that Muhammad passed on to his family? Were Muhammad's teachings and the blessings of God only to be found within the Qur'an and the emulation of the life of the Prophet and therefore available equally to all Muslims? If there was something special about Muhammad, then special consideration should be given to the Prophet's family in the political life of the new Islamic state. However, if the leaders of the Ummah should be chosen based on their knowledge of the Qur'an, their piety, and their ability to administer and defend the community, then there was no need to turn just to Muhammad's family for leadership.

Ultimately, those who believed in a special place for the role of the Prophet's family became the Shias, while those who believed that all Muslims were equally capable in the eyes of God became the Sunnis. Even today, however, many rulers claim lineage to the Prophet as a form of legitimacy, including in Sunni states such as the modern Hashemite dynasty in Jordan.[2]

Within the Shia position - that there is something unique about the Prophet's line that gives them a special ability to rule - there is an important division that was not immediately apparent

1   "Max Weber's Conceptualization of Charismatic Authority: Its Influence on Organizational Research" by Jay A. Conger in *Leadership Quarterly* V 4, I 3-4, pp 277-288
2   For the ancestry of the Jordanian Royal House, visit their official homepage: http://www.kinghussein.gov.jo/rfamily_hashemites.html

after the Prophet's death: is this uniqueness something that is born within them, or is it a special knowledge which comes from either a secret teaching or from insights gained from prolonged intimacy with Muhammad? This is important because if it is knowledge, then it can be codified and taught to those who are not his descendants, and it can also be lost by those who are.

While Muslims have continued to debate this issue, the Prophet and the Qur'an are ambivalent on it. On the one hand, there is a strong assertion of the equality of all Muslims, including the following passages:

> "O Mankind, We created you from a single (pair) of a male and a female and made you into nations and tribes, that you may know each other. Verily the most honored of you in the sight of God is he who is the most righteous of you (Quran 49:13)."

> "O people, Remember that your Lord is One. An Arab has no superiority over a non-Arab nor a non-Arab has any superiority over an Arab; also a black has no superiority over white, nor a white has any superiority over black, except by piety and good action (Taqwa). Indeed the best among you is the one with the best character (Taqwa). Listen to me. Did I convey this to you properly? People responded, Yes. O messenger of God, The Prophet then said, then each one of you who is there must convey this to everyone not present. (Excerpt from the Prophet's Last Sermon as in Baihiqi)"

> "The Prophet said: Let people stop boasting about their ancestors. One is only a pious believer or a miserable sinner. All men are sons of Adam, and Adam came from dust (Abu Dawud, Tirmidhi)."

On the other hand, these eminent sources also had something to say in support of the other side. There are a number of Hadith (sayings or teachings of the Prophet) that the Shia hold up to support their claims about Ali's special status as the heir-apparent of Muhammad. The first is the Hadith of the Pond of Kumm, when the Prophet gave a sermon in which he discussed how he would meet them in heaven: "I will ask you about the two weighty things that I have left for you when you come to me to see how you dealt with them. The greater weighty thing is Allah's book—the Holy Qur'an. One end is in Allah's hand and the other is in your hands. Keep it and you will not deviate. That other weighty thing is my family and my descendants."[3]

Another important argument is found in the Hadith of the Cloak, a story in which the Prophet wrapped Ali, Fatima and their two sons Husayn and Hasan in his cloak and declared that they were sinless and composed his family (and by extension were his inheritors). While there are a number of others, one that will come up later is the Hadith of the Twelve Successors, in which

---

3   The Sunnah of the Prophet can be found in English at: http://sunnah.com/

the Prophet taught that there would only be 12 legitimate Caliphs after him and a plethora of false caliphs, and that after the last of his successors the earth will end[4].

These religious interpretations remain an important part of the Sunni-Shia debate today, but in the early political context of the upheaval after the Prophet's death, these debates were not philosophical but were instead connected to different candidates for the mantle of Muhammad's successor. In fact, it is altogether possible that the candidates existed and were well-known before these justifications were developed to support them. Upon Muhammad's death, the debate was between two individuals: Abdullah ibn Abi Qhuhafah (commonly known as "Abu Bakr") and `Alī ibn Abī Ṭālib ("Ali").

4   *Muhammad: A Prophet for Our Time* by Karen Armstrong (2007)

A 16th century depiction of Abu Bakr in Mecca

Both men were already eminent within the Ummah and featured prominently in the histories of the Life of the Prophet. Abu Bakr was the father-in-law of the Prophet and - like Muhammad - was a merchant based in the city of Mecca before Muhammad declared his Prophethood. He was outside Mecca traveling with a caravan as Muhammad first announced his new faith, and when he returned to the city, Abu Bakr was the first convert to Islam from outside Muhammad's own family. This was a major step because Muhammad called upon Muslims to abandon narrow clan ties for connection to the larger Ummah, and Abu Bakr served as one of the Prophet's closest advisors. While his daughter Aisha was married to Muhammad, since the Arabs were (and remain) patrilineal, this meant that Aisha entered Muhammad's family (male line), but it also meant Muhammad did not enter Abu Bakr's family. As a result, Abu Bakr is not considered to be a kinsman of the Prophet.

Ali, on the other hand, was family. The cousin of the Prophet on the male line, he was also married to the Prophet's most beloved daughter, Fatima. According to Islamic histories, Ali was born in the Kaaba, the sacred shrine at the heart of the holy city of Mecca, and he was the first man to convert to Islam upon hearing Muhammad's message. Like Abu Bakr, Ali had served as the Prophet's lieutenant, especially in military matters. Ali had regularly led the Muslim troops into battle.

A 16th century depiction of Ali leading soldiers in battle

Chapter 2: The First Three Rightly Guided Caliphs

When the Prophet died in 632, choosing Muhammad's successor was a decision ultimately made by the Sahabah, a term used for the body of individuals who had known the Prophet during his life (in English, it is often called the "Companions of the Prophet"). It is difficult from such a distance to say exactly why the Sahabah preferred Abu Bakr over Ali, but there are several plausible arguments, and it's safe to assume that even Abu Bakr's supporters would have had different reasons for their allegiance to him. One is that Abu Bakr was considerably older than Ali, and in the strictly hierarchical society of Medieval Arabia, age and experience were vitally important. There is an old Arab saying that men are not wise until the age of 40,[5] and Ali was only 32 or 25 (depending on which source on his birth one reads).[6]

Another possible reason for excluding Ali from the center of power may have been based on the fact he was a member of the Prophet's family. Early Islam was a religion that placed a great emphasis on egalitarianism, especially since the Prophet and the Qur'an called upon Muslims to reject their old ties of clan, tribe, and ethnicity. It may have been that the Sahabah wanted precisely to avoid creating a hereditary dynasty within the Prophet's family as a supreme rejection of the old clannishness[7].

Whatever the reasons, Abu Bakr was chosen to become "caliph," a shortened form of the title "Khalifat Rasul Allah" ("Successors to the Messenger of God"). The Caliph inherited all of the Prophet's political authority and much of spiritual power as well.

Since the election of Abu Baker in 623, there have been hundreds of individuals from close to a dozen dynasties that have claimed the Caliphate, but only the first four are widely considered by Sunnis to have inherited the true spiritual mantle of the Prophet. These four men, all of whom were Sahabah (Companions of the Prophet in his life), are called the "Rashidun" (or "Rightly Guided" Caliphs), and their government is referred to as the Rashidun or Patriarchal Caliphate (632-661).

After the Prophet's death in 632, the Caliphate controlled the Arabian Peninsula, which today consists of Saudi Arabia, Yemen, Oman, the United Arab Emirates, and Qatar, but it expanded during the Rashidun period with the conquests of today's Iraq, Syria, Israel, the Palestinian territories, Jordan, Persia, Armenia, Egypt, Cyprus, Lebanon, Azerbaijan, Kuwait, and Bahrain, as well as portions of Afghanistan, Turkmenistan, Turkey, and Libya.

However, it was also during this period that the division between Sunnis and Shias was taking shape. Initially, it consisted of a political division, with the proto-Shia as something akin to a loyal opposition; they supported the overall system of the Caliphate, obeyed the Caliph's rulings and were pious Muslims, but they believed that Ali was the better candidate and may have had strong opinions about the special place of the family of the Prophet in public affairs.

One point of conflict during Abu Bakr's rule was over the oasis of Fadak. Located close to Mecca, it was one of the Muslim army's earliest conquests and had been under the direct control of Muhammad during his lifetime. At his death, his daughter Fatima (Ali's wife) claimed that it had been owned by Muhammad due to the right of conquest and that he had willed it to her. Abu Bakr, on the other hand, denied this claim and stated that a Prophet of God could not own property. Thus, Abu Bakr asserted that after the Prophet's death, the lands under his control

5   This is a widespread belief in Arab lands, and was confirmed by the fact that Muhammad's Prophethood did not begin until his fortieth year.
6   "The Caliphate" in *Islam: Faith, Culture, History* (2002). By Paul Lunde. DK Publishing.
7   *No God But God: The Origins, Evolution and Future of Islam* by Resa Aslan (2011). Random House

reverted back to public ownership and were to be managed by the Caliph. While Fatima assented to Abu Bakr's ruling, she was furious over it, and it created a rift between her family and the Caliph. After this event, Ali and Fatima retreated from the public eye to become farmers, but before she died a few months later, Fatima gave a rousing speech in the Mosque of the Prophet before the Caliph and the assembled Sahabah in which she denounced their government as turning its back upon true Islam and praising her husband as an alternative. This event, known as the "Fadakyiah Sermon," can be considered the intellectual foundation of Shia Islam, and it continues to resonate with Shias today.[8]

---

8   For a Shia interpretation of these events, read: http://en.shafaqna.com/etrat/item/26306-fadak-an-outcry-beyond-a-bequest.html

A medieval depiction of Muhammad giving Fatima in marriage to Ali

Fadak continued to emerge as a point of contention throughout the Rashidun Caliphate and became a symbol of the shoddy treatment that Shias believe the family of Ali and Fatima - the true heirs of the Prophet - received at the hands of jealous, power-hungry proto-Sunni Caliphs. It still continues to be a rallying cry for those who seek to restore the birthright of Ali's line, such as the radical Shia Fadak satellite television station, which broadcasts anti-Sunni rhetoric from London.

Abu Bakr only ruled for two years, and after his death, he was replaced by his handpicked successor, the famously stern Umar (also written Omar). Umar addressed Muslims in the wake of Abu Bakr's death and said, "O ye faithful! Abu Bakr is no more amongst us. He has the satisfaction that he has successfully piloted the ship of the Muslim state to safety after negotiating the stormy sea. He successfully waged the apostasy wars, and thanks to him, Islam is now supreme in Arabia. After Abu Bakr, the mantle of the Caliphate has fallen on my shoulders. I swear it before God that I never coveted this office. I wished that it would have devolved on some other person more worthy than me. But now that in national interest, the responsibility for leading the Muslims has come to vest in me, I assure you that I will not run away from my post, and will make an earnest effort to discharge the onerous duties of the office to the best of my capacity in accordance with the injunctions of Islam. Allah has examined me from you and you from me, In the performance of my duties, I will seek guidance from the Holy Book, and will follow the examples set by the Holy Prophet and Abu Bakr. In this task I seek your assistance. If I follow the right path, follow me. If I deviate from the right path, correct me so that we are not led astray."

Succeeding to the caliphate in 634, Umar ruled until 644 and profoundly shaped the emerging Muslim state largely through his skill as a jurist and lawmaker. Under Umar, the Caliphate continued to expand, conquering the Levant, Egypt, coastal Libya and - crucially for the future history of Shias - the entire Persian Empire. Umar attempted some reconciliation with the extended family of Ali, but he still maintained Abu Bakr's position on Fatima's contested inheritance at the oasis of Fadak.

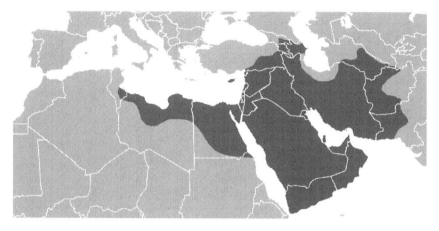

Mohammad Adil's map of the expansion of the Rashidun Caliphate

For the Sunnis, Umar has gone down in history as the greatest of the Faqih, an expert in "fiqh" (Islamic jurisprudence). During this period, the Ummah went through major changes as the number of Sahabah (Companions of the Prophet - those who heard Muhammad speak and had direct knowledge of his teachings) was decreasing both overall (as people like Abu Bakr died) and as a percentage of the overall population. This meant that the direct lessons of the Prophet and his example were becoming increasingly more difficult to teach, and as the Empire expanded, there was a greater need to apply Islamic law to an ever-growing number of cultural contexts. Umar and the scholars of his period began the process of collecting and codifying the Hadith (teachings of the Prophet) and creating a body of organized, universally-applicable laws for the new state[9].

While Sunnis and Shias differ on their interpretations of the Hadith, these collected sayings and acts of the Prophet are central to all forms of Islam and demonstrate how the word of God - the Qur'an - is applied in the life and words of a pious man as near perfect as a human could be. However, since the Prophet himself never wrote up a book of his teachings (Muslims consider the Qur'an a recitation from God given word-for-word to the Prophet), after his death there was a chaotic jumble of ideas. On top of that, the memories of the Sahabah began to falter as they grew older, and some Sahabah and non-Sahabah began to invent spurious "teachings."

What scholars have done for generations is collect and write down these Hadith and then sifted through the collections, examining the chain of oral transmission and the character of the transmitters to determine which Hadith they gave weight to. This also means that there are numerous similar (but often subtly or even dramatically) different versions of the same tale. The

9   *Islam: Faith, Culture, History* (2002). By Paul Lunde. DK Publishing. Pp 48-49

Sunni tend to be relatively liberal in accepting Hadith as their basic assumption; if a Sahabah reported a Hadith, they trust its veracity unless that individual can be shown to have abandoned Islam or the chain of transmission to the recorder was faulty. The Shia, on the other hand, interpret all of the Hadith through the prism of the treatment of the *Ahl al-Bayt* ("The People of the House"), a general term used for the descendents of Muhammad but used in Shia contexts only for Ali, Fatima and their descendents. Those among the minority that sided with Ali and Fatima against Abu Bakr and Umar in their disputes on inheritance and precedence are viewed by Shia faqih as the only legitimate sources of Hadith.

That said, during the era of Umar - before the open Sunni-Shia split - there were no such divisions made, so Muslim authorities were collecting Hadith not to compete with each other but to gather up the holy teachings before they faded from memory. In fact, at this point there were no theological differences between the proto-Sunni and the proto-Shia except for the relative importance they placed upon the political role of the Ahl al-Bayt, especially Ali.

In 644, Umar was murdered by a stab wound from a slave, and the fact that this slave was of Persian origin became a point of Sunni-Shia friction centuries later after Persia converted to Shi'ism under the Safavids. On his deathbed, Umar appointed a committee of six men to find his successor, and this committee included Ali and the eventual choice, Uthman ibn Affan. All six were part of the aging cohort of Sahabah and had been prominent political actors throughout the Prophet's reign and the succeeding caliphs.

The committee had to come to consensus, and according to legends, Umar ordered his son to kill any single member of the committee who held out against consensus. One of the six, Zubayr, backed Ali, and another, Sa'd ib Abi Waqas, supported Uthman. The remaining candidate/committee member, Abdur Rahman, withdrew from the running and was appointed arbiter. The final committee member, Talhah, was not present because he had been in a distant part of the empire when Umar died.

Eventually, the committee gathered before the Ummah at the Friday night prayers in the Mosque of the Prophet in Mecca, and when Abdur Rahman gave his support to Uthman, it forced Ali's hand. The committee announced it had reached a consensus, but Shias continue to maintain that Ali never accepted Uthman because he knew that the Prophet had appointed him as the only legitimate successor.

Regardless, upon his ascension, Uthman continued the military campaigns of his predecessor and pushed Islamic armies into Khorasan (today's northwestern Afghanistan), Balochistan (southern Pakistan), Armenia, and northern Africa. His rule lasted for 12 years, but while the first half of his reign was peaceful, the second half witnessed growing discord that eventually led to open revolt. The Shia argue that even in the time of Uthman, the later tendencies of the Sunni caliphs towards rule not as the first among equals but as dynastic monarchs was evident. Uthman had appointed his family members to governorships, accepted rich gifts, and used monies from the public treasury for himself, all of which flew in the face of the rigid egalitarianism of the previous rulers.

All of the discord culminated in 656 with the assassination of Uthman and unrest across the empire. The assassination itself was a dramatic event known as the "Siege of Uthman," which consisted of angry citizens/rebels from outlying areas converging on Mecca with a set of demands for Uthman. Central to their complaints was Uthman's appointment of his extended family as governors. The exact events are still unclear, but it is possible that documents were faked by his cousin Marwan (who would later be Caliph) that ordered the rebel leaders executed. Ali was called upon by Uthman to intercede, but his attempts at negotiations failed, so the rebels continued to besiege Uthman within his home. The siege was a slow-motion affair of many days and largely without open bloodshed - Ali was even able to bring water to the Caliph – but in the end, rebels led by Muhammed ibn Abu Bakr broke in and killed the Caliph[10].

Not surprisingly, the nature of these revolts and the assassination is clouded by centuries of assertions by Sunni and Shia, especially since the development of radical Wahhabi Sunni theology in the 19th and 20th centuries. The Wahhabis (who are discussed in much greater detail in the final chapter) argue that the decline of Islam is due to the corruptions of the true faith, in particular by the Shia, who they view as heretical. These theologians and historians argue that the Caliph was brought down by a Jewish figure named Abd Allah ibn Saba' al-Ḥimyarī, and that he was funded by external enemies of the Islamic empire to sow divisions within the faith and undermine the Caliphate. They argue that the theological roots of Shi'ism comes from this individual, who led a revolt movement that assassinated Uthman in order to put the corrupted Ali on the throne and end the Empire's expansion. The Wahhabis point to connections between some of the rebels and Ali, including Muhammed ibn Abu Bakr, who was Ali's adopted son[11] and became a general for him when he was Caliph.

Shia historians, on the other hand, claim that Abd Allah ib Saba' al-Ḥimyarī is a fictional character created to disparage the Shia by claiming that their theology is Jewish in origin. This is considered an especially damning charge after the creation of the state of Israel in 1948. Moreover, the Shias insist that Abd Allah ib Saba' al-Ḥimyarī was concocted to place the blame for the end of the Rashidun Caliphate on their betrayal[12]. Instead, they argue that the Caliphate lost its path when it appointed a figure other than Ali as Caliph in the first place, and that the creeping growth of this corruption could be seen in Uthman's increasingly monarchic tendencies.

In 656, Uthman's death finally made Ali the leader of the Caliphate, and respect for Ali and for

---

10 "'Uthman ibn 'Affan" in *The Encyclopedia Britannica* accessed online at:
   http://www.britannica.com/EBchecked/topic/620653/Uthman-ibn-Affan
11 The first Caliph, Abu Bakr, was his biological father.
12 For a summary of the evidence in the debate, read: "Authentic References and Case Research of ibn al Saba's Existence" accessed online at: http://makashfa.wordpress.com/2012/12/16/authentic-references-and-case-research-of-ibn-al-sabas-existence/

his caliphate is the last point of historical commonality between the Sunnis and the Shia before their trajectories took them in different directions. Changes had swept the Ummah (community of Muslims); the Prophet had died 34 years ago, and the community of his Companions - the Sahabah - were vanishing and losing their control over social and religious life. Thus, Ali took over an empire in the throes of revolt but managed to hold onto power for the next five years.

Immediately after the death of Uthman, the rebel factions declared Ali to be their Caliph, but Ali turned them down at first. As a result, the rebels demanded a Caliph be appointed, so the remaining members of the committee that appointed Uthman and were in Medina - Ali, Talhah, Zubayr[13] - met together in the Mosque of the Prophet with others of the Sahabah. This committee eventually appointed Ali the new Caliph, but there would be debate among those involved, as well as historians, as to whether this was done willingly or by force. Either way, the events at Medina were not unchallenged by those opposed to Ali, and conflicting rumors spread like wildfire across the Empire about the nature of Uthman's death and the appointment of Ali. The opposition gathered around Aisha, the Prophet's wife, and then around Muawiyah, the second cousin of Uthman and Marwan and the governor of Syria in Damascus[14]. Another lesser faction was based in Egypt around the governor of that province, Amr ibn al-As.

In one form or another, the First Civil War (called a "Fitna") consumed Ali's reign and ultimately brought about his death. Around him gathered a group of loyal followers who became known as the *Shī'atu 'Alī* , a term that means Party of Ali, and over time, "Shiatu Ali" became shortened to "Shia," the term that continues to be used today. Hence, it can be said that while the roots of Shi'ism go back to even before the death of the Prophet, the Shia become an identifiable political group upon Ali's succession.

The first open battle in the conflict was the Battle of the Camel on November 7, 656. When Muawiyah sent his word that he would not recognize Ali, Aisha, Talhah and Zubayr (who were on pilgrimage together) traveled to Medina to ask Ali not to attack Muawiyah but to instead hunt the killers of Uthman. When they learned that Ali was not hunting the killers, they allied with Marwan and his kinfolk (the Umayyad clan). Ali learned of their movements and summoned groups from the Iraqi city of Kufa to aid him.

When the two armies met, it seemed that conflict would be avoided once all of the main parties agreed to a truce and settlement. However, during that night, unknown hotheads attacked the camps, sparking wider fighting. Both Zubayr and Talhah refused to participate, but Zubayr was killed by one of his soldiers and Talhah was shot dead by Marwan. The battle was fierce and included thousands on both sides, with the focus being on the capture of Aisha on her camel. Aisha eventually surrendered and was pardoned by Ali, and Marwan was captured.

---

13 Sa'd ib Abi Waqas, was governing Persia at the time.
14 He was not, however, one of Uthman's nepotistic appointments as he had been given his position by Umar.

A medieval depiction of the Battle of the Camel

This solidified Ali's control over the heartland of the Caliphate but left the Umayyad clan and Muawiyah in rebellion in Syria. Thus, the civil war continued to rage as Ali attempted to conquer the rebellious provinces and hold the Caliphate together. Finally, the two armies met in 657 at the Battle of Siffin on the banks of the Euphrates River near present day Raqqa in Syria.[15] Once

---

15 There were roots of earlier conflicts here. The Byzantine and Persian Empires had long maintained proxy states in Syria and Iraq (respectively) and the two groups - both Arabic speaking - were old and bitter rivals even when

again, they were slow to engage and preferred to attempt to settle their difficulties, but even though the two sides held off for months to negotiate, fighting eventually broke out. Thousands died on each side and both leaders retreated, so the conflict remained unresolved.

Eventually, Ali agreed to Muawiyah's call for arbitration according to the laws set down in the Qur'an, but when word spread that Ali agreed to negotiations as if Muawiyah was an equal, a faction of his most radical and fiercest supporters broke off and retreated to southern Iraq, becoming a sect called the Kharijites. In the end, Ali left the arbitration greatly weakened, making Muawiyah the symbolic victor. Ali retreated to his wartime capital in Iraqi Kufa, and Muawiyah headed to Damascus, where he was declared Caliph in 658. There were other campaigns in the aftermath of Siffin, but Muawiyah's influence gradually began to expand. Ali was further weakened by battles in 659 against the Kharijites, which eventually led to his assassination by the Kharijites in the Great Mosque of Kufa in 661[16].

Chapter 3: The Umayyad and Abbasid Caliphates (661-1258)

After the death of Ali, his son Hasan was declared Caliph by his father's supporters, but by this time, the Shia were an increasingly Iraqi- based movement. Meanwhile, Muawiyah pushed hard, bringing first Egypt and then larger areas of Arabia under his rule. Finally, Hasan gave up and recognized Muawiyah's Caliphate.

Muawiyah broke from the traditions of the Rashidun by declaring that not only was he Caliph but that the position would be passed down within his family. In this way, the last egalitarian elements of the government were abolished and a new dynasty - the Umayyads - was established. The Umayyads would rule for roughly 90 years, and much of their state policy was conditioned by the Fitna, which included requiring all mosques to ritually "Curse" the name of Ali during Friday prayers for 60 years[17]. As a result, the Shia became a persecuted group with hidden followers scattered across the Islamic world, but they were mostly concentrated in Ali's old heartland of Iraq. The tomb of Ali in the Iraqi city of Najaf would become a center for pilgrimage, and the legend of Ali as a true Islamic ruler who was noble, just and forgiving would be taken up by Sunni and Shia alike. The weekly Cursing in the end only reinforced the pettiness and weakness of the Umayyads.

Once Muawiyah made his capital in Damascus, the seat of the Caliphate would never again return to the holy cities of Mecca or Medina, but for the majority of Muslims (the eventual Sunnis), it did not appear that there was a major break between the Rashidun and the Umayyads. After all, the first two Umayyad Caliphs had been prominent Companions of the Prophet and had

---

absorbed into the Islamic Empire. Hence, when Muawiyah went into rebellion in Syria, many Iraqis from Kufa were more than willing to join the fight against him.

16 "'Ali" in the *Encyclopedia Britannica* accessed online at:
http://www.britannica.com/EBchecked/topic/15223/Ali
17 A Shia analysis of these curses and original texts of them can be found at:
http://www.shiapen.com/comprehensive/muawiya/instituted-cursing-imam-ali.html

served prominently in the conquest and administration of the young empire. One of the four Rashidun, Uthman, had been a member of their clan, and they had all originated from Mecca itself. It was only many generations later, when the Umayyads had come to be seen as corrupt and nepotistic that the idea of the Four Rightly Guided Caliphs as separate from the Umayyads was promulgated and the concept that Ali was an ideal leader struck down by Umayyad treachery and double-dealing spread further.

As much as the Shia identity was forged through their persecution by the Caliphate and the nurturing of the cult of Ali and the veneration of his descendents as the true, hidden leaders of Islam, the Sunnis were also created by the Umayyad Caliphate. The entire Ummah had viewed the success of the early Islamic empire as evidence of God's blessing; obviously, if they had been able to conquer so far and wide and defeat ancient empires on the field of battle, then they must have special aid from the Lord. The Shia, obviously, came to distance themselves from the successes of the government as their persecution increased, but the Sunni also developed a new and complex relationship with the young state. They learned quickly during the Umayyad Caliphate that simply because a ruler declared themselves "caliph" and their empire was "Muslim," it did not mean the rulers were pious, just, or magnanimous. In fact, the famed cruelty, spinelessness and duplicity associated with the Umayyads may have been due to the disillusionment that any people expecting their emperors to be holy men experience.

While Sunnis continued to identify with the Empire and saw its successes as evidence of divine favor, they no longer expected their Caliphs to be true inheritors of the spiritual mantle of the Prophet. Instead, the best they came to hope for was that the political authority (the Caliph) would maintain stability, protect and promote Islam, and not grossly violate any of the laws of the Prophet. At the same time, since they still needed authorities to interpret the Qur'an and the Hadith, as well as administering the mosques and charities, a parallel Islamic hierarchy of Sunni religious figures arose, consisting of Muftis, Imams, Qadis and Khatibs.

Even as the Sunnis and Shias continued to split, there were still some overlaps between the two, and there have always been periods of shared history that they agree upon. One example is the 4th Shia Imam Muhammad ibn Ali (677–732), who, despite being the head of the "Party of Ali," became a well-respected scholar in Sunni circles as well. However, the simmering conflict between the Umayyad Dynasty and their Shia challengers to the throne exploded during the reign of the Caliph Yazid I, the son of Muawiyah I who reigned from 661-680. When Yazid came to power, he represented a new element in the religious and political life of the Empire; he was a ruler born after the death of the Prophet (and thus was not one of the Companions), and he was the first to be appointed to his position by filling his father's seat. Ali's son Hasan had ruled as Caliph for a short period during the conflict after his father's death, but this had not been over the majority of the Caliphate and was barely long enough for him to surrender. Thus, Yazid I came to represent the political corruption that was seeping into the Caliphate.

Ali's elder son, Hasan, had died in 670, so he did not live to see Yazid come to power, but his younger brother, Hussein (also spelled Husayn), did. In 680, Hussein had been the prominent leader of the Shia for 10 years, and he refused to accept Yazid as Caliph, noting that the peace treaty that he had signed with Muawiyah to end the Fitna had expressly prohibited the Umayyads from appointing one of their own as successor. Hussein was 54 at the time, while Yazid was only 34, and he had been one of the Companions of the Prophet. Furthermore he was mentioned by name in the Hadith, and the Prophet was said to have given him special favor. His most important ally at the time was ibn Zubayr, the grandson of Abu Bakr (the first Rasidun Caliph).

Hussein gathered his allies at Mecca, far from the center of Umayyad power in Damascus but at the heart of the old traditional power bases. The people of Kufa, Ali's old capital, heard of Hussein's revolt and sent word to Mecca that they were ready to join the revolution. They further encouraged him to make Kufa his capital, and against the advice of ibn Zubayr, Hussein gathered his family and companions and headed towards Kufa.

Meanwhile, Yazid moved quickly to consolidate his power, including sending his lieutenants to Kufa to depose the local governor and attempt to control the city's crowds. He also sent armies to the roads between Mecca and Kufa, anticipating Hussein's movements. Once Yazid's forces encountered Hussein on the road, there was a tense period of negotiation and wary watchful encampments. According to Shia accounts, Hussein's party shared water with the Umayyad soldiers, but they refused to return mercy by forcing Hussein to encamp far from water sources and then killing Hussein's younger brother, Abbas. Both sides agree that the truce broke down, resulting in the Battle of Karbala, during which Hussein and 72 of his followers were killed and decapitated. The bodies of the dead were left in the desert, but the soldiers returned with the heads and the captured women and children to Damascus to deliver them to Yazid. In the process, Hussein's sister Zaynab rose to prominence by denouncing the Caliph and protecting the honor of the surviving female members of the family.

A depiction of important figures at the Battle of Karbala, with the central figure being Abbas

These shocking events were seared into the consciences of the people of Kufa and all of the Shia, not to mention many Sunnis who have come to view the Umayyad Dynasty as corrupt and tyrannical. The annual observance of Hussein's death is called Ashura, meaning "Tenth," referring to the fact that it is the 10th day of the Muslim month of Muharram. For the Shia, it is seen as a day commemorating triumph over, and opposition to, tyrannical government. According to legend, the first commemoration of Hussein's death was held in the prison in Damascus and led by Zaynab, who has since become a symbol of strength, resistance to oppression, and piety.

Eventually, a mosque – the Imam Husayn Shrine – was built in Karbala over the grave of Hussein, and it became the focal point of annual Ashura pilgrimages, but even outside of Karbala, Ashura has become a time when Shia march through the streets of their hometowns carrying banners, funeral biers, and performing an act called a Matam, which involves beating one's breast either with the open palm or holding an object like a knife or a chain, in lamentation for the dead. Ashura is the most obvious, public, and controversial marker of Shia identity, and the annual celebration of Ashura is always fraught with controversy and conflict. For one, it is a symbol of Shia-ness in nations where the Shia are often a minority (such as in India or Lebanon) or an oppressed majority (such as in Saddam Hussein's Iraq or contemporary Bahrain). On the other side, it is a symbol of opposition to oppression and has become a rallying point for dissent against tyrants (such as the Shah of Iran, Saddam Hussein or the government of Pakistan).

The Imam Husayn Shrine in Karbala, Iraq

Some Sunnis also observe Ashura, though not as dramatically as their Shia neighbors. In addition to its association with Hussein, who is respected in some Sunni circles as a pious opponent to Yazid's corruption of Islam, it is also believed to be the date when Moses led the Israelites out of Egypt and is therefore an important date associated with the tyrannical pharaoh's fall. Today, Ashura is a state holiday in Iran, India, Afghanistan, Turkey, Pakistan, Iraq, Azerbaijan, and Lebanon, only some of which have Shia majorities[18].

The Umayyad dynasty was relatively short-lived, lasting from the end of the Fitna in 661 until 750, a span of 89 years, but during this time, they held the single Muslim Caliphate together as a political entity and extended its borders into Spain and Portugal, the Sindh (today's southeastern Pakistan), the Maghreb in Northern Africa, and the Caucasus Mountains, making it one of the largest empires the world had ever seen. As with any large empire, there was considerable unrest across the caliphate, especially with the Umayyads becoming increasingly unpopular amongst Muslims and non-Muslims alike. This led to the Second Fitna (Civil War) in the 680s and 690s as well as the Berber Revolt in the 740s. The Berber Revolt opened a period of increasing instability and weakness, leading to the Third Fitna (744-747), increased taxes, declining central control, and finally the Abbasid Revolution of 750.

---

18 "The Umayyads" in *Islam: Faith, Culture, History* (2002). By Paul Lunde. DK Publishing. Pp 50-53

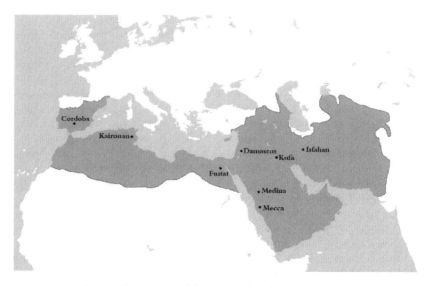

A map of the extent of the Umayyad caliphate at its peak

The Abbasids were Muslims but, for the first time, they appealed to a wide, non-Arab population base. Just as the Prophet Muhammad had left an unresolved tension over how the Ummah was to be ruled after his death, there was also a tension between the universal nature of the faith and the special place of the Arabs in it. On the one hand, it was obvious that his prophetic mission was to the Arabs, especially since he dictated the Qur'an in Arabic and insisted that it never be translated into another tongue, and he had also said that other prophets had come to other peoples but that he was sent to the Arabs and the vast majority of his early followers (the Companions) had been Arabs. At the same time, however, he also preached that he was the last Prophet and the one sent to bring the final, perfect message of God to all of humanity, and he made speeches that were opposed to paying too much attention to narrow family-based loyalties and similar tribal or ethnic identities. In the years after his death, as the Empire continued to expand, there was an ongoing debate of sorts as to whether Islam was a faith for Arabs or for all of the peoples of the Empire, especially since they tolerated other monotheistic faiths like Christianity, Judaism and even Zoroastrianism. Furthermore, if others did convert to Islam, would that mean that they needed to "convert" to being Arabs and speak Arabic? Even as other peoples began to convert to Islam, there was a sense among many of them that they were second-class Muslims in the eyes of Umayyads, and this was especially true among the people of Kufa.

As for the Abbasids, they were Arabs who claimed descent from Muhammad's uncle, Abbas (hence the name "Abbasid"). The Abbasids gathered support in the northeastern regions of the Empire, particularly in Khorasan and Persia, where people called for a return to governance by the House of Muhammad (the "Hashemite" clan). The revolution began during the reign of the Umayyad Caliph Marwan II, the 14th of his line. He ruled from 744-750 and witnessed the Persian-speaking provinces of Persia and Khorasan, as well as the Shia of Kufa and other areas of the Empire, rise up behind Ibrahim the Imam, the great-great-grandson of the original Abbas. Ibrahim was killed in 747, but his next-oldest brother, as-Saffah, continued the revolt and overthrew the government in 750. He declared his status as Caliph in 749 in a speech in Kufa, where he made his first capital, a demonstration of the connection to the Shia movements based in Kufa that had always promoted the reign of the family of Muhammad over other forms of government. His younger brother, al-Mansur, became the second caliph and moved the capital to a new city of his own construction: Baghdad.

The Abbasids would rule directly - both politically and spiritually - over the Muslim Empire from 750-1258, a period which is considered by many to be the Golden Age of Islam and the period when the Caliphate was the intellectual center of the known world. Another important development was the greater integration of Persians into the administration of the Empire and their growing involvement in Islamic arts and letters. However, the Caliphate as a political unit fell in 1258 when the Mongols sacked the city of Baghdad and integrated most of the Empire into their own empire. The Abbasids fled to Cairo, where they served as the symbolic religious leaders of Islam, but political power was wielded by their military officers, a caste called the Mamluks. The Abbasids continued there in a symbolic capacity until Cairo was conquered by the Ottomans in 1517[19].

Chapter 4: Development of the Shia After the Death of Hussein

During the later years of the Umayyad reign, the Shia also continued to develop along their own trajectory. After the death of Hussein in the Battle of Karbala, his only surviving son - Ali ibn Hussein (659 - 712) - was a weak and sickly young man whose life had been spared out of mercy. Said to be the son of Hussein and a Persian princess named Shahrbanu (his mother died when he was young), Ali ibn Hussein was not a warrior leader like his father, grandfather or great-grandfather, but he was a man of learning. Ali ibn Hussein reconstructed the school in Medina that Muhammad had founded, and he wrote a series of important texts. Shia have traditionally blamed his death upon poisoning at the hands of the Umayyads, and he was buried in Medina.

19   "The 'Abbasids" in *Islam: Faith, Culture, History* (2002). By Paul Lunde. DK Publishing. Pp 54-58

A picture of Ali ibn Hussein's tomb before it was destroyed

   His son, the Fifth Imam, Muhammed ibn 'Ali al-Baqir (676 - 733), officially renounced political aspirations and became a renowned teacher of Islamic law in Medina. For this reason, he is often given the title "Baqir al-'Ulum" ("Revealer of Knowledge") or just "al-Baqir" ("The Revealer"). He organized schools, taught students directly, spearheaded the compiling of books of law and Hadith, and generally promoted learning within the Empire. It is said that Shia from Kufa and elsewhere secretly traveled to Medina to listen to his teachings, but like his father, he is said to have been poisoned by the Umayyads and was buried in Al-Baqi' Cemetery alongside his father. Al-Baqi' became a place of important pilgrimage for Shia and all who venerated the family of the Prophet, as those buried there include the Imams Hasan, Ali ibn-Husayn, Muhammed ib Ali al-Baqir, his son Jafar, the Caliph Uthman, Muhammad's uncle Abbas (founder of the Abbasid line), Muhammad's daughter Fatima, a son of Muhammad who died while still an infant, and all but one of his wives.

The sixth imam was Ja'far ibn Muhammed al-Sadiq (702-765), who was also a jurist in Medina like his father and grandfather. Jafar codified the previous teachings and is considered to be the founder of a distinctly Shia school of jurisprudence named for him: Jafari Jurisprudence. He ruled during a period of disintegration and rebellion against the Umayyads, a conflict which he remained largely aloof from even though many of his kinsmen died, and he is said to have rejected the Caliphate when it was offered to him and instead claim the position of Imam. He then attempted to remain neutral and continue teaching during the new Abbasid Caliphate, but when he died in 765, it was widely believed he was poisoned by the second Abbasid Caliph, Al-Mansur (founder of Baghdad).

In the chaos after Jafar's death, the Shia split into two factions that are now called the Twelvers and the Ismailis. The Ismailis were followers of Jafar's eldest son, Ismail ibn Jafar (719 - 760?), who is believed by most to have died before his father (though his followers instead claimed that he had gone into hiding from the Abbasids). The Twelvers supported the third son of Jafar, Musa al-Kadhim (745-799), who continued the family tradition of teaching in Medina until 795, when he was imprisoned by the Caliph in Baghdad and was held for five years until he was poisoned.

This pattern continued for some time. Imams (as the Shia leaders were called) lived in Medina, teaching their students and serving as a pious, peaceful counterexample and potential dynasty-in-waiting to the Abbasids, only to be poisoned by agents of the Caliphs (at least in Shia recollections of the events). This was true of the Eighth Imam Ali ibn Musa (765-817), the Ninth Imam Muhammed ibn Ali (810-835), the Tenth Imam Ali ibn Muhammed (827-868) and the Eleventh Imam Hassan ibn Ali (846-874).

The Ismaili Imam Muhammed ibn Ismail (740 - 813), on the other hand, based himself at first in the Shia bastion of Kufa and appears to have taken a more secretive and more political direction. His successors, the Eighth, Ninth and Tenth Ismaili Imams, also remained in hiding in Kufa to avoid being poisoned. There, in the shadow of Abbasid power in Baghdad, they gathered followers and power, extending networks of influence throughout the Empire until the Eleventh Imam, Al Madhi, would be able to rise to power as the leader of the Fatimid Caliphate in the early 900s.[20]

Chapter 5: The Final Split and the Fatimid Caliphate

Until the end of the 9th century, the differences between the Sunnis and Shias had been primarily political in nature. The Sunnis had supported the Umayyad and Abbasids (or at least tolerating their rule as a relatively benign necessity), while the Shia supported the Imams descending from the Prophet Muhammad via his daughter Fatima and cousin Ali. However, religious differences had continued to accumulate throughout that time as they developed

20 A summary of the Ismaili position on the history of the Imamate can be found here at the Aga Khan's homepage: http://www.akdn.org/about_imamat.asp

different interpretations of jurisprudence, especially after the Sixth Imam, Jafar, created Jafari Jurisprudence. Sunni Islam also had its own different schools of jurisprudence.

While the different schools of jurisprudence may not have been a sticking point, the theology of the main branch of Twelver Shia broke away from this shared tradition due to an event in 874 known as the Occultation. The Shia Imams had often led shadowy lives over the centuries as they faced oppression, but they also served as lightning rods for political opposition to the dominant caliphates. For the secretive and far-flung Shia communities, the Imam was not just a flesh-and-blood political or religious leader but also a symbol of true nobility, piousness, and resistance in the face of oppression.

The final historic Imam in the Twelver school of Shia was Muhammad al-Muntazar, the Twelfth Imam, who is also called "Muhammad al-Mahdi al-Hujjah" or "Muhammad al-Mahdi." Born in 869, he ascended to the position at the age of five upon the death of Hasan al-Askari, his father and the Eleventh Imam. Hidden away by his followers, the Imam communicated with the outside world through a series of appointed spokesmen, the "Four Deputies." For seven decades, this system remained in place until - right before the death of his fourth and final deputy - he sent a letter to his followers around the Muslim world declaring that he was withdrawing from this world and would be hidden by God until the time of the Lord's deciding, when he would return to aid the Shia. Pious Twelver Shia thus believe that today, some 12 centuries later, the Hidden Imam remains and awaits his return to the world and his judgment of humanity. Furthermore, they believe that the Twelfth Imam is al-Mahdi, the promised Messiah whose return will herald the End of Days.

The concept of an Imam hidden by Occultation had been relatively common in the various smaller sub-branches of Shia Islam, so it was not a new theological concept. However, the emergence of the Occultation signaled a major shift in the nature of Shia Islam, and it was the last step in a long, slow process of political withdrawal by the Twelver Shia. Originally a political movement promoting a particular dynasty to control the Caliphate, by this time it no longer possessed a physical ruler to take the throne but had become its own theological and spiritual path. This also freed up Twelver Shia to be adopted by other rulers and other dynasties as their own, in particular the Persian dynasties of the Safavids and Qajars[21].

In conjunction with the development of the theology of the Occultation and the foundation of Twelver Shi'ism, another branch of Shia was also making great strides in the 9th and 10th centuries: the Ismailis. After the death of the 6th Imam, Jafar, the Shia split between the followers of the son of his elder son Ismail (hence the term "Ismailis") and the followers of his third son, Musa. The followers of Musa remained based in Medina and developed an intellectual strand of Shi'ism around their clerical Imams that eventually lead to the Occultation. The

---

21 "Muhammad al-Mahdī al-Hujjah " in *The Encyclopedia Britannica*, accessed online at:
http://www.britannica.com/EBchecked/topic/396330/Muhammad-al-Mahdi-al-Hujjah

Ismailis, on the other hand, took a more political approach to their Imamate, based out of the restive Shia city of Kufa.

In 899, the Eleventh Ismaili Imam, Abdullah al-Mahdi Billah, left Arabia to travel to North Africa, where agents of his father had found allies amongst the Berber peoples. In 905, he was captured by local authorities, but his followers led a Berber army to free him in 909, after which he assumed control of the nascent state and declared himself Caliph. His armies went on to win a string of spectacular successes, conquering modern-day Algeria, Tunisia, Libya, Egypt and portions of Morocco. Eventually, the dynasty settled in Egypt and founded a new capital, Cairo, in 969. Like the Abbasids in Bagdad, the new dynasty – which called itself "Fatimid" after their ancestor Fatima, the daughter of the Prophet – wanted a new, wholly-Muslim capital city to rule over and to replace the Christian capital of Alexandria.

Thus, from 909 onwards, there were two rival caliphates: a Sunni Caliphate in Baghdad led by the Abbasid Dynasty (descending from Muhammad's uncle Abbas) and a Shia Caliphate in Cairo led by the Fatimid Dynasty (descending from Muhammad's daughter Fatima and from the Imam Ali). Further complicating the picture was the fact that remnants of the old Umayyad Dynasty established themselves in parts of Spain, where they created their own Caliphate based in Córdoba in 929.

The Fatimids reached their peak in 1069, when they held all of North Africa, the Sudan, the Levant, and the Holy Cities of Mecca and Medina, and within this region, they maintained a remarkable level of religious tolerance, including allowing Sunnis to rise to political office. Eventually, however, the Fatimid power was weakened by the betrayal of the Berbers to the Abbasids, the Crusades, and Turkic invasions of the Levant. They finally fell to the great Sunni sultan Saladin in 1174, and Saladin recognized the Abbasid's religious authority.

An illustration depicting Saladin

Before they fell, the Fatimids also established the mosque and madrasa of Al-Azhar in Cairo. This center of learning drew upon not only Muslim traditions but also Greek Christian scholars from Alexandria and eventually Jewish scholars as well. It became the most important center of learning for the Fatimids, but after Saladin's conquest of the city, it was converted over to Sunnism. After the Abbasid Caliphs moved to Cairo in 1261, Al-Azhar became associated with the learning of the Caliphate and became the single most important Sunni institution in the world, a position it retains today.

Daniel Mayer's picture of Al-Azhar

At its height, the powerful Fatimid Dynasty was the only true challenger to Sunni political domination of the Islamic world after the death of Ali, and this period has colored Sunni-Shia relations ever since. The prolonged Fatimid/Abbasid Wars have provided tales of outrages and fuel for hatred, as have the dark fears among Sunnis that if the Shia ever rose to political power, they will once again threaten the Sunni political heartland of Arabia. Among the Shia, this period drove a wedge between the Ismailis and the Twelvers. The Ismailis have since taken a more religiously tolerant and political tone (the current Ismaili Imam – the Aga Khan V – is a cosmopolitan figure who seems more like a jet-setting prince than a religious leader). They also have been deeply influenced by Greek philosophy (Gnosticism, Pythagoras, Aristotle and others) from their time controlling Alexandria and Cairo, even though they have since moved as far away as the mountains of eastern Tajikistan. Meanwhile, the Twelvers (who were the minority in the Fatimid period), maintained a more scholarly, inward-looking, and mystical approach, one that drew strength from its politically-weak, minority position.[22]

Chapter 6: The Safavids in Persia and the Ottomans in Turkey

For the Abbasids, the Shia Imams always presented an existential threat, but unlike the Umayyads, who justified their rule based upon military victory and the righteousness of the selection of the Caliph Uthman (and his inglorious death), the Abbasids relied upon the Shia argument that their ancestry within the clan of the Prophet Muhammad and direct descent from his uncle Abbas gave them special authority to rule. At the same time, however, it was undeniable that the Shia Imams held the better claim to rule by being descended directly from the Prophet via his favorite daughter Fatima and his beloved, pious and gallant son-in-law and cousin, Ali. Thus, by arguing for their own legitimacy, the Abbasids also made a strong case for the legitimacy of the Imams. This led to mutual suspicion and the oppression of Shia, especially after the rise of the rival Fatimids. Once the Fatimid dynasty began to gain power, the scattered Shia communities within the lands of the Abbasid Caliphate came to be viewed as potential fifth columns within their communities.

The Sunni-Shia conflicts that characterized this period ended abruptly in 1258, the year the non-Muslim Mongols invaded the Abbasid Caliphate and conquered the city of Baghdad. The previous collapse of the Fatimid Dynasty meant that there was no powerful Shia political force to move into the vacuum, so the two Islamic camps came to a mutual accord in order to unite against an outside force. This invasion shook the Sunnis in particular to the core, as it was the first time that their Empire was seriously threatened by a non-Muslim force and the first time that they could not point to the military successes of the Islamic Empire as evidence of God's grace.

Despite having a common enemy, the era of tolerance broke down once again when the Shia regained a political footing. In the far north of the Islamic world, in the city of Ardabil (in today's Iranian Azerbaijan) near the Caspian Sea, a semi-secret order of mystical Sufis called the Safaviyya had existed since the late 13th century. The Safaviyya Order grew in prominence throughout the region and slowly morphed from promoting Sufism (a mystical outgrowth of Sunni thought) to Twelver Shi'ism. In the 1400s, the Order gained a militant aspect and began to build a territorial base for itself, and in 1501, Ismai'il, the leader of the Order (which had been an inherited position for centuries) eventually declared himself "Shah." His new empire was Twelver Shia in character, and the resulting dynasty was called the Safavids.

The Safavids went about recreating the territory of the ancient Persian Empire that had been conquered by the early Rashidun Caliphate, and at their height, the Safavids controlled all of today's Iran, Armenia, and Azerbaijan, as well as large areas of Iraq, Afghanistan, Kuwait, Georgia, Turkey, Syria, Pakistan and Turkmenistan. The Safavids forcibly converted the lands under their rule to Twelver Shi'ism, and also promoted – for the first time in centuries – Persian

---

22 "The Fatimids" in *Islam: Faith, Culture, History* (2002). By Paul Lunde. DK Publishing. Pp 59

pride and identity. After centuries of Arab political dominance, the Persians enthusiastically embraced the new identity and, after a time, were willing to fuse their ethnicity with the Shia religion.

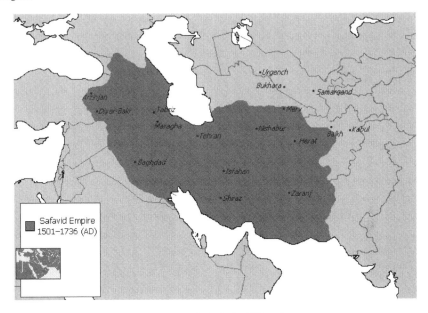

The extent of the Safavid Empire

As the Safavid dynasty emerged, the Ottoman Empire as the standard bearer for Sunni Islam.[23] A rising power for generations, the Ottomans reached the status of world power in 1453 when they conquered the city of Constantinople (today's Istanbul) and set themselves up in the heartland of the old Byzantine Empire. This position was reinforced in 1517 when the Ottomans conquered Egypt, deposed the Abbasid Caliphs, and claimed the Caliphate and control of the holy cities of Mecca, Medina and Jerusalem for themselves.

Naturally, the two powers quickly took up the geopolitical positions of the old Byzantine and Persian Empires in the time before Islam and fought over much of the same territory, including Mesopotamia, the Caucuses, today's eastern Turkey and the Persian Gulf. Their first battle was fought in 1514, their first real war was fought from 1532-1555, and they continued to spar regularly until the early 19th century, when European colonialism forced them both onto the defensive. Echoes of these conflicts can be seen in the recent sparring between Iran and Turkey

---

23 The other great Muslim empire of the age, the Mughals in India, were officially Sunni, but were deeply influenced by Shia and Persian thought and never took up Sunnism with the same vigor as the Ottomans.

through proxies in Iraq and Syria.

Much has been made of the brutality of the Safavid conversion of the Persians and the savagery of the conflicts in general, especially amongst Sunni fundamentalist authors who use the term "Safavid" as an insult to describe any pro-Shia Iranian force. It appears that the Safavids sought to convert Persia for several reasons, not only out of a true religious fervor dating back to their days as a secret religious brotherhood but also in order to heighten the differences between their Empire and the Ottomans and prevent fifth column loyalists to the Ottoman Caliphs from undermining their empire. It is important to note that while the Ottomans did not need to convert their population to Sunnism, they used religion just as cynically and showed just as little mercy towards the Shia in their lands as the Safavids did to the Sunni. Moreover, while some states (like the Fatimids) demonstrated a great tolerance within their empires, this was an age of relatively unmitigated brutality and intolerance on the part of all sides.

Regardless of how merciless each side was in comparison to the other, the rise of these two Empires drew an even firmer line between the Sunnis and the Shias, and they provided fresh atrocities for both sides to cite. It also served to catapult Twelver Shi'ism from the political margins to the forefront of the Shia world and, crucially, permanently associated Shi'ism with Iran and the Persians.[24]

Chapter 7: The Split in Recent History and Growing Anger

Since the final collapse of the Islamic Empires in the 19th and early 20th centuries at the hands of the Europeans, relations between the Sunnis and Shias have become even more embittered. The anger has grown prevalent across the Muslim world, and the Shia have borne the brunt of the religious violence over the past 30 years. History has shown that Sunni-Shia violence tends to increase when the Shia have some political power (such as during the Safavid and Fatimid dynasties) and when the Sunnis themselves feel weakened, and this has been the case with the rise of the Islamic Republic of Iran.

Perhaps the most important development in the differences between the Sunni and the Shia in modern history has been the development of a new school of thought in Sunni religiosity: Salafi or Wahhabi Islam. The Wahhabis date their history back to the mid-18th century, when an Arab thinker named Muhammad ibn 'Abd al-Wahhab (1703-1792) developed a new theology that violently rejected what he saw as the corruption of Islam and the growing Christian domination of the Muslim World. Looking for a source of the ongoing scandalous humiliation of the Muslim world, he looked inwards to flaws within the Ummah. According to al-Wahhab, if the Muslims were the chosen people of God, their subservience to Christians was not due to Christian superiority but due to God withdrawing his favor because the Muslims had turned

---

24 *Islam: Faith, Culture, History* (2002). By Paul Lunde. DK Publishing. Pp 68-73

away from Him. In this worldview, the goal of the modern Islamic community should be the rejection of corruption and perversion and a return to the true, pure faith of the Prophet and his Companions.

This faith - a return to the "fundamentals" of religion - is a form of fundamentalism and is remarkably similar to Christian, Jewish and even Hindu fundamentalist movements that also emerged around the globe in the late 19th and early 20th centuries[25]. In all of these faiths, the believers understand what they saw as the political or social inferiority of true believers as evidence that the deity or deities had withdrawn their favor from a faith that had rejected the fundamentals of their religion. All of these religions sought to purify the faith by removing what they understood as corruptions, superstitions, and perversions, but the process, while claiming to be traditional has been a profoundly modern one that has violently rejected much that defined the traditional faith.

Al-Wahhab allied with Muhammed bin Saud, the founder of the state of Saudi Arabia, and provided religious and ideological backing to the newly formed state. The Wahhabi Saudi troops took advantage of the chaos of the collapse of the Ottoman Empire after World War I to seize control over the holy cities of Mecca and Medina. It's probably safe to say that the Shia will never forgive the Wahhabis for the zealotry they pursued upon taking the cities, which included obliterating centuries-old sacred Shia shrines and claiming that they were used to worship the Imams as gods and were therefore heretical. In the Cemetery of al-Baqi in Medina, they utterly destroyed the tombs of the Imams Hasan, Ali ibn Husayn, Muhammed ibn Ali, and Jafar, as well as the tomb of Fatima, the daughter of Muhammad. In Mecca, they destroyed the Cemetery of Mualla, where the ancestors of Muhammad and his first wife Khadija were buried. These prominent destructions were part of a pattern of violence that witnessed the Wahhabi Saudis smash buildings, tombs and mosques associated with the history of the Prophet and his family and which were venerated by Shia. In addition, they alienated Shia from governance and oppressed them throughout the kingdom[26].

This vandalism has been repeated time and time again by Wahhabis in other areas as well, including the much-publicized destruction of the Buddha statues of the Bamiyan Valley of Afghanistan by the Taliban in 2001[27] and the outbreak of violence in 2013 around the city of Timbuktu, where Wahhabi fundamentalists destroyed holy artifacts and burned a priceless library of manuscripts before fleeing the arrival of French troops[28].

---

25 *The Battle for God* by Karen Armstrong (2001)
26 "History of the Cemetery of Jannat Al-Baqi" accessed online at: http://www.al-islam.org/history-shrines/history-cemetery-jannat-al-baqi
27 UNESCO has put together a gallery of the destroyed Buddhas, available here: http://www.unesco.org/new/en/media-services/multimedia/photos/bamiyan-photo-gallery/
28 "Timbuktu's Treasure Trove of African History" (2013) by the BBC Online. Accessed online at: http://www.bbc.com/news/world-africa-21242689 and "Islamists Destroy Door of Ancient Timbuktu Mosque" in the *Egypt Independent* newspaper (2013). Accessed online at: http://www.egyptindependent.com/news/islamists-destroy-door-ancient-timbuktu-mosque

While the establishment of the Wahhabi school of thought created an intellectual form of anti-Shia ideology, it is probable that this philosophy would have remained isolated in the political backwater of the Nejd Sultanate (the core of modern Saudi Arabia) if not for the fall of the Ottoman Empire and the final abolition of the Caliphate. The Ottomans had claimed to be Caliphs of the Muslim world since 1453, the same year that they conquered Constantinople (Istanbul) from the Byzantine Empire, and they ruled over a considerable portion of the world's Sunnis, as well as the shrine cities of Mecca, Medina and Jerusalem. After 1876, the Sultans had placed particular emphasis on their role as Caliphs in order to bolster their global position by asserting their Empire's "Muslim" character, and while this was never universally accepted by all Sunnis or Shias, Sunni Muslims everywhere at least could say that there was a government that claimed to represent the form of rule established by the Prophet and that provided legitimacy and continuity.

However, after the end of World War I, the Ottoman Empire was devastated. The French had claimed Syria, the British had Iraq and the Mandate of Palestine, and the Greeks, Armenians and Italians were attempting to carve up large sections of Anatolia for their own states. A brutal series of wars began in which the secularist Turkish nationalist factions of the army, led by Mustafa Kemal Atatürk, drove their enemies from Turkish Anatolia. Atatürk's government declared Turkey to be a secular republic in 1923 and finally abolished the institution of the Caliphate in 1924. The end of the Caliphate, accompanied by the twin currents of Turkish-style secular nationalism (referred to as "Ataturkism" by its detractors) and European colonialism, untethered the political fortunes of the Sunni Muslims from a traditional power base and left many of them feeling lost and powerless[29].

---

29 A summary of his secular philosophy can be found at: http://www.allaboutturkey.com/ata_prensip.htm

Atatürk

The abolition of the Caliphate was important for modern Sunni-Shia relations, but perhaps the most influential event of the 20th century was the 1979 Islamic revolution in Iran. During that Islamic revolution, the ancient dynasty of the Shahs (which claimed to have ruled Persia for 2,500 years) was overthrown by a coalition of forces that eventually became dominated by the Shia ulama (the priesthood), especially the Grand Ayatollah Ruhollah Khomeini.

Khomeini

This event resonated within the Sunni communities for several reasons. First, it demonstrated that an Islamic revolution was possible, and that modern Islamic governments could be established and resist the counter-revolutionary forces arrayed against it. Furthermore, Iran became the first state in generations that was an ardent international supporter and promoter of Shia Islam. With that, neighboring Sunnis feared the growth of Shi'ism among their people, a sentiment that is still very much alive across the Middle East.

Khomeini and his government attempted to downplay the Sunni-Shia divide whenever possible, and this has been the general policy of Iran ever since. The Iranians instead attempted to focus Muslim attention upon the Israeli-Palestinian conflict and the ongoing intervention of the West in the affairs of Muslim countries, with the goal of creating an outside enemy that both Sunni and Shia could unite against. Iran has also sought to promote the Islamic Revolution outside of Iran, even amongst Sunnis, which includes financing Hamas, a Sunni group, in the Palestinian territories. The Iranian ulama has gone out of its way to reach out to open-minded Sunni clerics, endorsing the Sunni position (though not Wahhabism) as legitimate forms of Islam and asking the Sunnis to do the same.

At the same time, it cannot be denied that the mere existence of a Shia state has galvanized Shia militants and created new tensions across the region. This has fueled the political opposition of the two Wahhabi states, Saudi Arabia and Qatar, and led them to fund anti-Shia groups in Pakistan, Afghanistan, Syria, Iraq and elsewhere. The ongoing struggle for Shia strength in Lebanon, Iraq, Yemen and Syria is opposed everywhere by this powerful coalition of Sunni forces, which consists not just of official states but also shadowy terrorist groups and political networks[30].

As a result, any attempt to understand the ongoing conflicts and antagonism must begin with the religious character of the states involved. Shia Iran is currently fighting the Islamic State, a Sunni group, in Iraq, which has a Shia majority. Meanwhile, Iran has also helped prop up the Syrian government led by Bashar al-Assad (an Alawite whose sect is associated with Twelver Shia), who is still fighting a civil war against Sunni rebels financed by nations like Sunni Saudi Arabia. Iran and Syria have both historically been primary sponsors of Hezbollah, a Shia militia of considerable strength in Lebanon.

In this sense, the Sunni-Shia divide has become the most prominent political fault line across the Muslim world, with traditional Sunni nations like Saudi Arabia and Egypt on one side against Shia powers like Iran and Syria. With no sign of change on the horizon, it seems the divide between the two main branches of Islam will continue to be increasingly relevant in the future.

Bibliography

Ahmed, Akbar (1999). Islam Today: A Short Introduction to the Muslim World (2.00 ed.). I. B. Tauris. ISBN 978-1-86064-257-9.

Bennett, Clinton (2010). Interpreting the Qur'an: a guide for the uninitiated. Continuum International Publishing Group. p. 101. ISBN 978-0-8264-9944-8.

Brockopp, Jonathan E. (2003). Islamic Ethics of Life: abortion, war and euthanasia. University of South Carolina press. ISBN 1-57003-471-0.

Esposito, John (2010). Islam: The Straight Path (4th ed.). Oxford University Press. ISBN 978-0-19-539600-3.

---

30 *The Shia Revival: How Conflicts in Islam will Shape the Future* by Vali Nasr (2007). WW Norton Company

Esposito, John (2000b). Oxford History of Islam. Oxford University Press. ISBN 978-0-19-510799-9.

Esposito, John (2002a). Unholy War: Terror in the Name of Islam. Oxford University Press. ISBN 978-0-19-516886-0.

Esposito, John (2002b). What Everyone Needs to Know about Islam. Oxford University Press. ISBN 0-19-515713-3.

Farah, Caesar (2003). Islam: Beliefs and Observances (7th ed.). Barron's Educational Series. ISBN 978-0-7641-2226-2.

Firestone, Reuven (1999). Jihad: The Origin of Holy War in Islam. Oxford University Press. ISBN 0-19-512580-0.

Goldschmidt, Jr., Arthur; Lawrence Davidson (2005). A Concise History of the Middle East (8th ed.). Westview Press. ISBN 978-0-8133-4275-7.

Hawting, G. R. (2000). The First Dynasty of Islam: The Umayyad Caliphate AD 661–750. Routledge. ISBN 0-415-24073-5.

Hedayetullah, Muhammad (2006). Dynamics of Islam: An Exposition. Trafford Publishing. ISBN 978-1-55369-842-5.

Hofmann, Murad (2007). Islam and Qur'an. ISBN 978-1-59008-047-4.

Hourani, Albert; Ruthven, Malise (2003). A History of the Arab Peoples. Belknap Press; Revised edition. ISBN 978-0-674-01017-8.

Kramer, Martin (1987). Shi'ism, Resistance, and Revolution. Westview Press. ISBN 978-0-8133-0453-3.

Lapidus, Ira (2002). A History of Islamic Societies (2nd ed.). Cambridge University Press. ISBN 978-0-521-77933-3.

Lewis, Bernard (1984). The Jews of Islam. Routledge & Kegan Paul. ISBN 0-7102-0462-0.

Lewis, Bernard (1993). The Arabs in History. Oxford University Press. ISBN 0-19-285258-2.

Lewis, Bernard (1997). The Middle East. Scribner. ISBN 978-0-684-83280-7.

Lewis, Bernard (2001). Islam in History: Ideas, People, and Events in the Middle East (2nd ed.). Open Court. ISBN 978-0-8126-9518-2.

Lewis, Bernard (2003). What Went Wrong?: The Clash Between Islam and Modernity in the Middle East (Reprint ed.). Harper Perennial. ISBN 978-0-06-051605-5.

Lewis, Bernard (2004). The Crisis of Islam: Holy War and Unholy Terror. Random House, Inc., New York. ISBN 978-0-8129-6785-2.

Madelung, Wilferd (1996). The Succession to Muhammad: A Study of the Early Caliphate. Cambridge University Press. ISBN 0-521-64696-0.

Momen, Moojan (1987). An Introduction to Shi`i Islam: The History and Doctrines of Twelver Shi`ism. Yale University Press. ISBN 978-0-300-03531-5.

Nigosian, Solomon Alexander (2004). Islam: its history, teaching, and practices. Indiana University Press.

Peters, F. E. (2003). Islam: A Guide for Jews and Christians. Princeton University Press. ISBN 0-691-11553-2.

Rippin, Andrew (2001). Muslims: Their Religious Beliefs and Practices (2nd ed.). Routledge. ISBN 978-0-415-21781-1.

Sachedina, Abdulaziz (1998). The Just Ruler in Shi'ite Islam: The Comprehensive Authority of the Jurist in Imamite Jurisprudence. Oxford University Press US. ISBN 0-19-511915-0.

Smith, Jane I. (2006). The Islamic Understanding of Death and Resurrection. Oxford University Press. ISBN 978-0-19-515649-2.

Teece, Geoff (2003). Religion in Focus: Islam. Franklin Watts Ltd. ISBN 978-0-7496-4796-4.

Trimingham, John Spencer (1998). The Sufi Orders in Islam. Oxford University Press. ISBN 0-19-512058-2.

Turner, Colin (2006). Islam: the Basics. Routledge (UK). ISBN 0-415-34106-X.

Turner, Bryan S. (1998). Weber and Islam. Routledge (UK). ISBN 0-415-17458-9.

Waines, David (2003). An Introduction to Islam. Cambridge University Press. ISBN 0-521-53906-4.

Watt, W. Montgomery (1973). The Formative Period of Islamic Thought. University Press Edinburgh. ISBN 0-85224-245-X.

Watt, W. Montgomery (1974). Muhammad: Prophet and Statesman (New ed.). Oxford University Press. ISBN 0-19-881078-4.

Weiss, Bernard G. (2002). Studies in Islamic Legal Theory. Boston: Brill Academic publishers. ISBN 90-04-12066-1.